This Book Belongs To:

_____

$a = 0.75 - 0.25 * float$

$a = 0.75 - 0.25 * float$

void()<hello>

void()<hello>

float

Published 2019, by Torchflame Books
an Imprint of Light Messages Publishing
www.lightmessages.com
Durham, NC 27713 USA
SAN: 920-9298

Hardcover ISBN: 978-1-61153-327-9
Paperback ISBN: 978-1-61153-325-5
Library of Congress Control Number: 2018966478

BUGZERO.CODES
BRINGING KIDS TO TECH

EVERYONE CAN CODE
(INCLUDING KIDS)

Timothy Amadi

Illustrations by Quillor Studios: quillor.com

I give all the praise to the Lord
for this gift He has given to me,
and on this day, I dedicate this
book to Him.

I am grateful.

1 You see, a chef she may

2 use coding in a way

3 that helps people buy food

4 any time of the day!

```
if (isFoodReady(food) === true) {alert ('Ready')}
```

5   A teacher, in turn

6   can code if they yearn

7   to provide their class

8   with a fun way to learn!

```
if (isSpelledCorrectly(word) === true) {alert ("Correct!")}
```

9   A nurse who learns quick

10   can code a good trick

11   to help out her patients

12   before they get sick.

```
if (isPatientSick(findings) === true) {alert ('Patient is S
```

13   A plumber who thinks

14   can code in a blink,

15   so he will know how

16   to fix a clogged sink.


```
if (isSinkClogged(status) === true) {alert ('Need to fix!')}
```

17   A bus driver who's cool

18   can code a new tool

19   to know how many kids

20   to pick up before school!

```
if (countStudentsOnBus(totalOfStudents) === true) {alert ('
students have been picked up!')}
```

21   A policeman in time,

22   can code on a dime

23   to help find new ways

24   to fight against crime!


```
if (isThereAnEscapeRoute(map) === true) {alert ('Block all es
routes.')}
```

25   A firefighter can wire

26   a code to inspire,

27   and find new ways

28   to fight against fire!

```
if (isThereAFire(fire) === true) {alert ('Need a firefighte
```

29 A doctor himself

30 may learn coding in stealth,

31 and find ways to boost

32 his patients' good health!

```
if (isPatientHealthy(findings) === true) {alert ('The patient
great health!' )}
```

33 A writer may look

34 to code in a nook,

35 so she has a new way

36 to write a great book!

```
if (isGrammarCorrect(sentence) === true) {alert ('The gramm
is correct!')}
```

37   A zoologist who's new

38   can learn to code too,

39   to show people animals,

40   they can't find in a zoo.

```
if (isAnimalInTheZoo(animal) === false)
{alert ('Not yet in the zoo! Take a picture and record it!')}
```

41 An electrician might learn

42 to code late at night

43 so he can make sure

44 you have plenty of light.

```
if (isWireCut(wire) === true) {alert ('Wire is Cut!')}
```

45   A dentist might mean

46   to be a coding machine

47   so he can make sure

48   your teeth stay healthy and clean.

```
if (isCavity(tooth) === true) {alert ('Cavity')}
```

49   A farmer named Joe

50   learned to code with a glow

51   to make sure all of his

52   crops would indeed grow!

```
if (isPestInCrop(crop) === true) {alert ('Crops have pests'
```

53 "That's right guys!" I say.

54 "Now let's have some fun.

55 Let's bring the gift

56 of coding to everyone!"

57 "Remember, coding is not

58 just for the few.

59 Everyone can code.

60 Even kids just like you!"

```
if (canICode(myage) === true)
{alert ('Yes you can! There is no age limit in coding!')}
```

About the Author

Coding is the global language of today's digital world, so I want to encourage kids to learn how to write code for themselves.

Kids can learn to identify challenges and build solutions to problems around their homes, schools, and communities through coding.

I continue to be driven by a passion for coding. As I learn more, I am better able to give back to other kids and through them to communities around the world.

It is always a pleasure to be invited by schools to motivate boys and girls to find solutions to needs around them through code. I like to encourage each one to understand that they, too, can code.

Besides coding, I love to play ping pong, the xylophone, and the piano.

Acknowledgments

Daniel and Eugene, I want to tell you thanks for the long run.

Thank you, Mr. Obi. You've been amazing.

Mr. Cole, we have come a long way.

Mr. David, I still remember our first meeting. You believed I could do it.

Miss Adkins, thank you for being my best friend when I needed it.

Mrs. Joyner, thank you for the conversation you had with my mom! Thank you for introducing me to Philip.

Philip, I still remember that one meeting we had when you told me that if I wanted to make an app, I had to first learn how to code. Thank you for that information. It started a new journey.

Dede and Mrs. Parchue, thank you for all your support.

Thank you, Mr. Small. You have taught me so much. I look forward to the time we spend together.

All my A+ teachers at school, I love you all.

Thank you to my church family. You have all had a big impact on my life.

Auntie Joyce and Auntie Uche, you mean everything to me.

Grandma, thank you for all the help you've given me.

Mom, I LOVE YOU. You sat with me in every class in my coding school. You have made so many sacrifices for me. I would have been nowhere without you.

```html
<!DOCTYPE html>
<html>
<head>
<title>Everyone Can Code Including Kids</title>
    <meta charset="UTF-8">
    <meta name="description"
    content="Everyone Can Code by Timothy Amadi"
    <meta name="keywords" content="Coding">
    <meta name="author" content="TimothyAmadi">
    <meta name="viewport"
    content="width=device-width,
             initial-scale=1.0">
</head>
<body>
    <h1>About BUGZERO.CODES</h1>
    <p> Hi, we are Timothy, Eugene and Daniel.
        No matter what you do or how old you ar
        everyone can code.
        Follow us on our coding adventure
        at www.bugzero.codes
    </p>
</body>
</html>
```

www.ingramcontent.com/pod-product-compliance
Lightning Source LLC
Chambersburg PA
CBHW081306040426
42452CB00014B/2668